Magic
A Treatise on Natural Occultism

By
Manly P. Hall

Illustrations by M. D. Logan

ISBN: 978-1-63923-159-1

Printed: February 2022

Cover Art By: Paul Amid

Published and Distributed By:
Lushena Books
607 Country Club Drive, Unit E
Bensenville, IL 60106
www.lushenabks.com

ISBN: 978-1-63923-159-1

Magic
A Treatise on Natural Occultism

By
Manly P. Hall

Illustrations by M. D. Logan

PART ONE

The Children of the False Darkness

1. For ages man has labored under a misunder-
standing. He has called the perversion of occult power
black magic. This is an improper use of the word
black, for black does not mean evil. Black is the basic
not-color of all things; it is the source of all being and
represents the body of the Absolute Intelligence. All
consciousness and light is born out of the chaotic blackness, and Kosmic Night with its dark *pralaya* is the
Father-Mother of creation. Black darkness must forever shroud the workings of the Infinite, and no matter how much light there is in the human soul, it is
forever surrounded with the dark seething substances
of Chaos. All manifestation is a concretion of dark
and unmeasured possibility.

2. The *Children of the Dark Birth* who labor in the
blackness of this substance, molding it into myriads of
unseen and unmeasured forms, are not evil. They are
the sons of Saturn (Satan) the Black Father who, like
the very darkness of Chaos itself, must in time swallow
all of his creations and in so doing bring them back to
life again from the death that men call creation. We
are all born out of this dark abyss and have no right
to call it evil. It is the parent of Gods and men—forever wrapped in the unexplorable robes of its own
mystery. Out of this blackness, Nature's unfathoned
treasure-house, man must exhume the stone of his own
soul in the same way that the miner removes the dia-
mond from its sheath of black carbon.

3

3. The dark *Lords of Saturn* are the builders of the first dawn, the morning of blackness, and from the friction of their strivings were born the first flaming sparks of dawning consciousness. They were the Mind-born and are the Brahmins of our chain of globes, being delivered from the brain and mouth of Brahma. Their throne is made up of solid substance and the chemicals of solid matter. They are the Satanic outpourings, the spirits of cold darkness.

In the diagram that follows are shown the four births which have come out of the body of Brahm (BrAUM) the Unknown Blackness, the x of Being:

5. There is a false darkness and a true darkness. The true darkness is the womb of Light; the false darkness, the perversion of the light that pours out of the true darkness. Natural darkness is the basic principle of things, while the false darkness is the result of debasing the power of the angels of Satan.

6. The Devil, the archetype, of misuse, is not a son of Saturn but is a *son of man* and the false darkness of earth. Man is the incarnation of the germ of mental intelligence and black magic is possible only to intelligent beings.

7. *Absolute spirit* minus all the sheaths of vehicles, unformed and uncompounded, is true Darkness—the dimensionless basis of all that is, has been, or ever shall be, and the ultimate veil behind which all creation must retire.

8. *Absolute crystallization* is the false darkness and is the colorless vibration at the lower end of the spectrum opposing the colorless vibration at the upper end of the spectrum. Both ends ultimately are swallowed up in darkness: one in the darkness of spirit and the other in the darkness of matter.

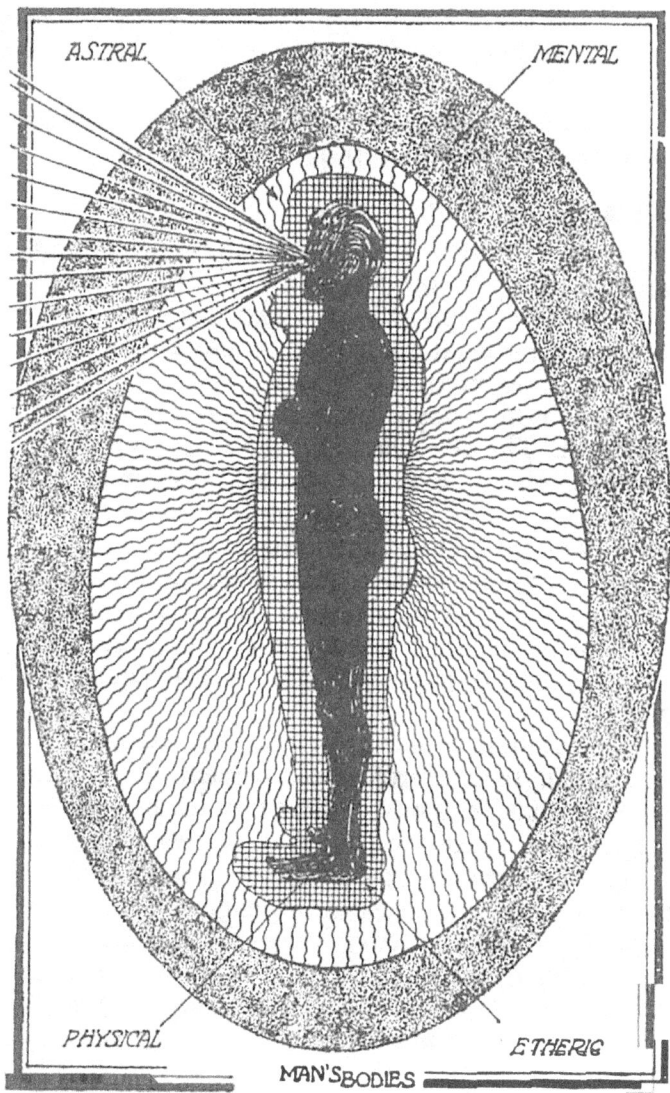

ASTRAL

MENTAL

PHYSICAL

ETHERIC

MAN'S BODIES

5

9. Life lives in darkness and dies in light; form lives in light and dies in darkness *but in dying really comes to life,* for life as we know it is pure death.

10. Natural darkness is unawakened possibility; false darkness is perverted opportunity.

The Philosophy of Opportunity.

11. If it were not for opportunity in its various forms there would be no perversion of power. There is an old saying: "Opportunity makes the thief." Opportunity is the eternal temptation; without temptation there could be no sinners. Therefore, when the higher powers brought man opportunity they also brought him sin and death. *The one who brought him Light brought him also the false darkness.* Light and shadow are inseparable; the shadow of light is the false darkness, for the creation of the first automatically brings the second. To be free from temptation man must be free from reason; to be free from darkness he must renounce light. Thus he becomes a renouncer of opposites, for in accepting one opposite he must needs accept the other.

12. *Temptation is the price that the human race pays for intelligence;* therefore the Serpent of Wisdom is also the eternal Tempter. When man learns with his growing intelligence of the powers of Nature and, most of all, of the power that he himself possesses, there comes with that increasing knowledge ever greater responsibilities. If man today knew of the god-powers that lie dormant within him he would be the most dangerous creature in the universe, both to himself and to the plan of things. *The soul must grow with the knowledge that it gains, otherwise the organisms will ultimately destroy each other.* Action and reaction must build strength of character so that the

6

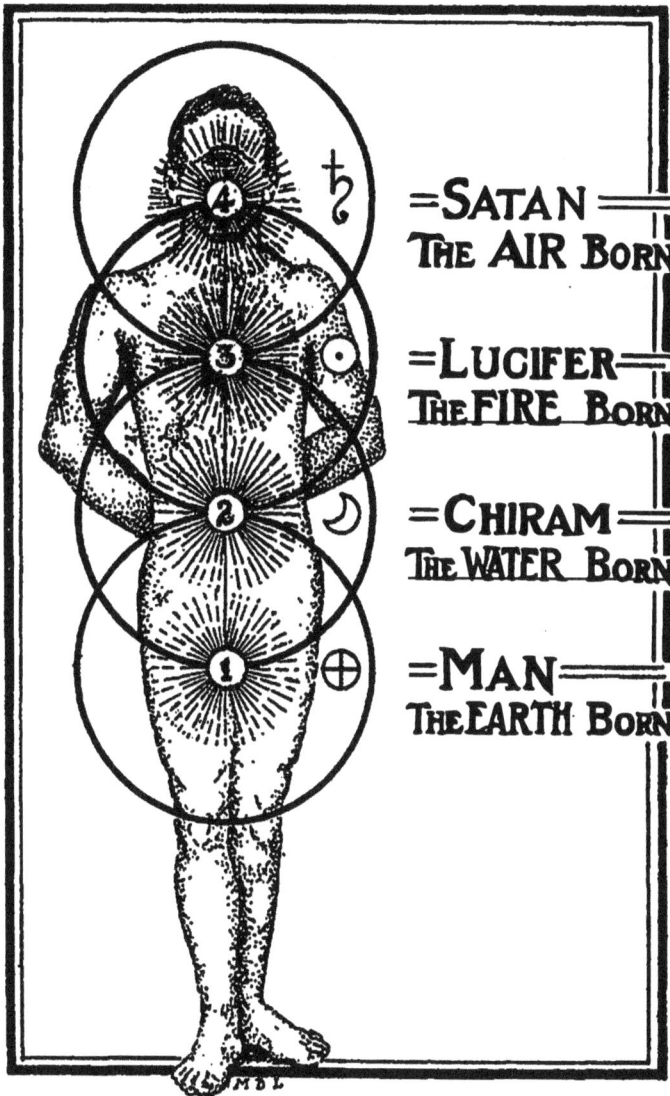

=SATAN=
The AIR Born

=LUCIFER=
The FIRE Born

=CHIRAM=
The WATER Born

=MAN=
The EARTH Born

THE MACROCOSMIC MAN
THE FOUR BIRTHS OUT OF THE BODY OF
BRAHMA

will is always strong enough to curb the desires. When this is not the case and desire runs rampant, then, regardless of the position of the organism in the path of unfoldment, a black magician is created.

13. Man has no free will at the present time, but merely the power of choice over a certain area of incidents brought by his ever-growing consciousness within the scope of his comprehension. These incidents have been differentiated by his evolving organisms from the dark *primum hyle* or the true blackness. The greater his growth, the larger the area of his choices and the greater his independence.

Why has been the eternal question in Nature, and the letter Υ is its phonetic equivalent, for it forms the sling that hurls the white stone at the forehead of Goliath. The latter represents the false darkness, while the stone represents true illumination.

14. In Egypt the point where the arms of the Υ converge was called the forking of the ways. The candidate for spiritual things always stands at the point where the three arms of the Υ come together, carrying in his hand the scales of discrimination. As long as he measures blindfolded, his weights will be just; but woe unto him if he removes the blindfold, for the two eyes themselves give birth to good and evil.

15. The diagram accompanying this paragraph shows the Υ of choice passing upward through the four creations of Brahma. The line passing through the circle shows the path of evolution through those kingdoms of Nature where there is no conscious reason—therefore no revolt against the laws of God. The small ring where the three lines meet shows the present position of the human ego dwelling in the mind of Brahma. From it the path branches. *Man must*

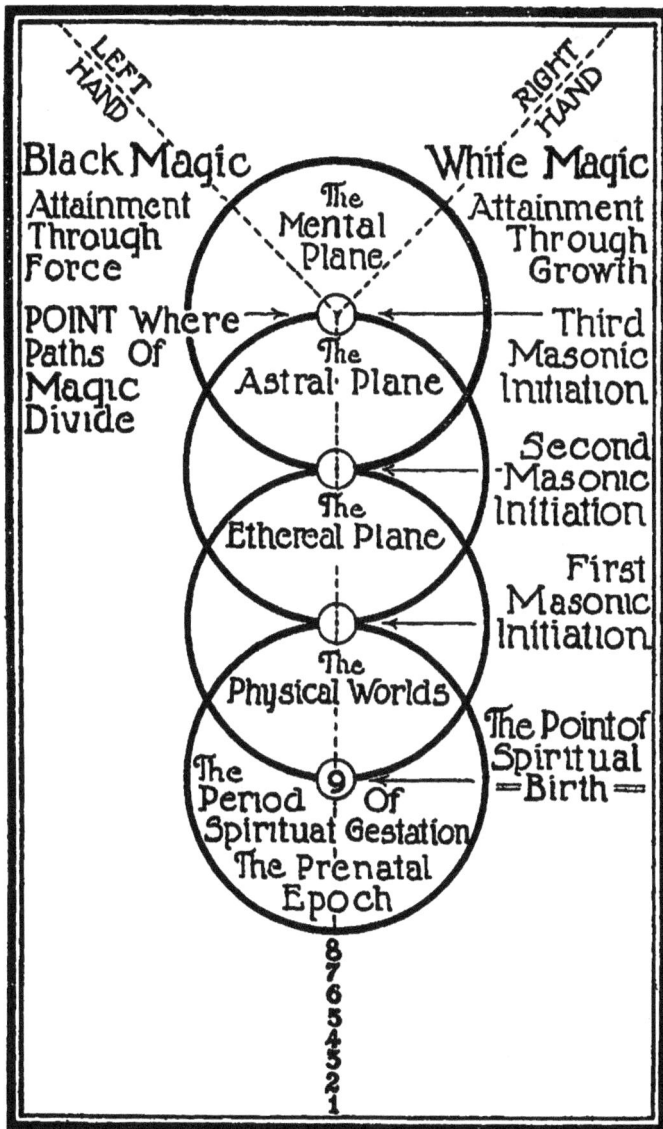

LEFT HAND

RIGHT HAND

Black Magic
Attainment Through Force

The Mental Plane

White Magic
Attainment Through Growth

POINT Where Paths Of Magic Divide

The Astral Plane

Third Masonic Initiation

Second Masonic Initiation

The Ethereal Plane

First Masonic Initiation

The Physical Worlds

The Period Of Spiritual Gestation
The Prenatal Epoch

The Point of Spiritual = Birth =

9

8
7
6
5
4
3
2
1

THE PATH OF HUMAN PROGRESS, AND THE
FORKING OF THE WAYS.

now choose his own way instead of depending upon Na-
ture. He has in spirit and in truth reached the point
where the scales of Libra have been inserted by cut-
ting the sign of Scorpio-Virgo in two and thus dividing the way of unfoldment.

16. During the first half of this fourth globe the
Great Ones came to man to strengthen him for his
choice and to give him basic instructions through which
he should learn to redeem his own soul. We know
these demigods now only as mythological characters;
but they were the ones who labored with the human
mind while it was in the making and planted therein
the seeds of *discrimination,* which is the ultimate Re-
deemer of human reason.

17. Those who follow the right-hand path enter
into one of the seven rays which lead to immortality;
while those who follow the left-hand path enter the
ray that leads to ultimate crystallization. Both lead to
darkness—one to the immortal darkness of divine union
and the other to the mortal darkness of divine annihil-
ation. The accompanying diagram may make this point
clearer:

THE POWER OF CHOICE

God's greatest gift to man and the cause of all suffer-
ing—the Hope of Immortality.

The Left-Hand Path.

THE FRUITAGE OF BLACK MAGIC

Those who take this path (No. 1) choose that their
immortal spirits shall be the servants of lower bodies,
in this way involving themselves in ever denser mater-
iality and enmeshing their consciousness more and
more in matter. If this practice is persisted in long

enough, the spirit will be unable to disentangle itself from the substances of the lower worlds and must remain enmeshed therein until the dissolution of the universe at the time of the Night of Brahma when the divine spark is cast back into the blackness of the Infinite through the rings of Saturn. By taking this path the Ego attains darkness, but it is the darkness of the tomb and of unconsciousness reached through the path of perversion and negation. Its reward is the *Black Death* and the loss of the soul. Such an Ego wanders in a great Unknown without hope, reason or understanding, while the endless wheels of Chaos dissolve the bodies of which it has failed to make the proper use.

The Right-Hand Path.

THE FRUITAGE OF THE WHITE MAGIC

In taking this path (No. 3) the spirit identifies itself with those who choose to liberate the divine essence

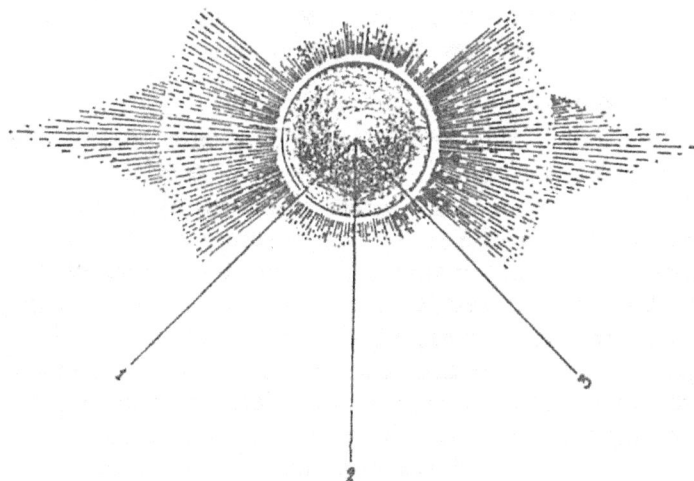

from its bodies and to have them for servants rather than masters. The consciousness unwinds itself from matter in a spiral motion and functions in ever finer substances until it completely disentangles itself from form and consciously attains the resurrection. In so doing it gains the powers to mold matter into whatever forms are necessary for its labors. It crosses over into the worlds of spirit and in so doing enters what man can know only as darkness. Light is a form emanation and when we enter the Divine Presence we enter the Omnipotent Darkness. This is the living Shade over which we have perfect power and which contains within itself all things in unawakened potentiality. We have allied ourselves with the *Dark Cause*, the womb of Light and have become molders of the Kosmic scheme.

Path No. 2 represents the non-existing spiritual equator dividing the poles, and is that ridge which divides the black and the white paths, like that mystic line which separates day from night. In this the spirit ignores opportunity, rejects reason and in this way comes under the law and mystery of—

The Mechanics of Opportunity.

18. All action immediately sets into motion the law of reaction, which the ancients have called the law of Karma, which is the factor employed by Nature for the creation of the soul. The rejecting or ignoring of opportunity, falling under the law of indifference and inertia, fails to result in a reaction. This, in turn, results in the starving of the soul. Those who have ignored experience are called the soulless creations and are in the same position as those kingdoms which, like the angels, have not been given individual intelligence. The law of reaction immediately starts incor

porating into the organisms the fruitage of the out-
poured endeavor, in this way slowly transmuting the
entire chain of vehicles into intelligent symbols or
images of the path chosen by the consciousness. As one
pole or the other slowly grows within the being, the
atoms of the opposing substances are slowly crowded or
forced out or sloughed off for lack of cohesion. The
battle of these opposing qualities in the various organisms of life forms the groundwork for the great
war of India or the Armageddon of Christian theology.
Through this subtle process the student, living the
white path, slowly starves out or else transmutes the
powers of the black ray within himself—that is, if he
is able to stand the conflict which must first take place
in his bodies. On the other hand, the student who
takes the black path slowly eliminates or destroys all
of the finer principles within until he becomes a very
demon incarnate. Once having destroyed conscience,
he does evil for the joy of it.

Definitions of Magic.

Magic is the art of manipulating the unseen forces of
Nature.

A Magician is one who is capable of *juggling* the
four elements of bodies.

A Magician is one who is capable of consciously
molding the substances of matter of the three and a half
worlds of material substance.

19. A White Magician is one who is laboring to
gain the confidence of the Powers That Be and to
prove through the purity of his life and the sincerity
of his motive his worthiness to be intrusted with the
great Arcana (the Wand of the Magus.)

A Black Magician is one who seeks to gain authority
over-spiritual powers by means of force rather than by

13

merit. In other words, he is one who is trying to storm the gates of heaven; he is one who is seeking spiritual power and occult dominion with an ulterior motive.

The Black Magician's motto is: "Might is Right" (survival of the fittest.)

The White Magician's motto is: "Right is Might" (survival of all.)

Grey Magic is the unconscious or subconscious perversion of power.

Yellow Magic is the failure to learn how to prevent the perversion of power.

Black Magic is the use of spiritual powers to gratify animal or selfish proclivities.

White Magic is the right use of spiritual power, consciously and objectively.

20. Every living person is in one of these four classes. It is important that each should analyze himself and see just which class he is in. There is nothing in all the universe so subtle as the powers of false darkness. We must go over our lives every day, for we never reach a place of safety. The more power we have, the greater light we have, the stronger the temptation to abuse it or to use it for self-gratification. We must learn to realize that the greater the knowledge the greater the penalty for abusing it. The sin that is excusable in the child is unforgivable in a man. *Motive.*

21. Motive is the key to the problem of Magic. Even the greatest of White Magicians can become a degenerate in an instant if his motive becomes unworthy. The White Magician serves humanity; the Black Magician seeks to serve himself.

22. The Black Magic of the past, the darkness that sank Atlantis when man made slaves of the demons of the elements and chained them to do his bidding, still survives to this day. The Black Magic of the Middle Ages with its witchcraft and orgies is not dead; only its form has changed like all other forms in Nature. It has incarnated again in our age with all its power and fury. It is gnawing as in the days of old at the very heart of our civilization and if left unredeemed will tear down and destroy our race. Under the garb of right it masquerades as the messenger of the Most High, yet under its oral promises forever lurks the menace of the Goat of Mendes. In its false shadows hide the furies of hell and the vampires of the astral plane.

23. As the Black Magician has no legitimate means of securing his power, not having passed through the school of reclamation, he wanders the earth like the werwolves of old, vampirizing humanity to secure the vitality which he must have to continue his operations.

24. All who are not consciously fortified in the path of right are possible victims of these monsters of iniquity; all who are not consciously on the white path and firmly established in the way of sincerity and truth are in eternal danger of these harpies who float like soulless spectres on the tide of evolution. They have the powers of invocation and demons who serve them, while the impartial natural law is misused hourly that they may perpetuate themselves. The power of light in their hands becomes but a sceptre of death, for many hands wield spiritual powers whose hearts are dead, whose minds are rotting dens of iniquity and whose souls have long since bid them good-bye. They are lost beyond recall to this life wave for they have killed out even the germ of good within themselves.

They battle on, however, clinging desperately to life at any price, realizing only too well that eternity holds nothing for them.

May the mercy of God rest upon them.

The End of the First Instruction.

SPIRIT

G
O
D

D
O
G

MATTER

Spirit is matter inverted and
matter is spirit inverted.
The beast is God defiled.

PART TWO.

The Power of Demons

The Source of Power in Magic.

25.   All occultists realize that there is but one source of vitality in the universe and that is the emanation ring of the Universal Logos. This power is not split up until it reaches the lower worlds where it grades itself according to vibratory rate. Magicians, both Black and White, draw their power from the same great stream which pours eternally from the center of the Causal Being and spreads along the lines of the radius to the circumference. The difference between Black and White Magic lies not in the force used, which is always divine power, but in the manner that it is secured and employed. The source of the Black Magician's power is said to be the Devil, to whom the infernal conjuror must sell his soul in exchange for the cooperation of this evil spirit in the attaining of his nefarious ends. In order to clarify this problem, let us analyze the composition of the Devil, who is in reality the most abused creature in the universe, for man through his perversion of divine energy is eternally transmuting his own deity into a demon.

The Personality of Evil.

26.   For many ages theologians have insisted upon personalizing natural principles. All the great forces of being are dressed up like puppets in a Punch and Judy show and have the pronouns *him* or *her* applied to them. This is one of the main reasons for the in-

ability of theologians to read the Bible correctly or intelligently. They are unable to see the abstract power under the concrete symbol. For ages religion has made the Devil a human being and, incidentally, human beings devils. This is incorrect, both in principle and application. The Devil is a natural principle, the product of natural means, and the ultimate of natural perversion. The Devil is a compound-complex creature, dividing himself up into all the sins of the calendar. Studied as a group entity first, the Devil is the spirit of perversion or negation, the created principle of misuse.

27. Evil is not a false thing; there are no false things in the creation of a true God. Evil is an abuse or misuse of power. It is the crossing of currents or an interference with the plan. We may say, as one definition of evil, that it is the right thing in the wrong place. The worst evil in Nature can be transmuted into good by the simple process of adjustment. The average intelligence of the consciously functioning man is sufficient to make a god out of any demon by the simple process of inversion; likewise he is capable of making a demon or evil thing out of any good thing or god by placing it in improper relationship to other things. The word *Devil* is used to cover the two excesses of polarity in Nature, for when uncurbed, either will destroy the organism that man is seeking to construct.

The Two Great Demons of Creation Are:

SATAN—SATURN

28. Satan is the spirit of caution, prudence, and when perverted, negation. At his door are laid the sins of omission. Few realize that man is responsible

for the things he has not done. That is part of the law. It is just as wrong not to do the right things as it is to do the wrong thing. Satan inhibits, he draws back, he holds aloof. He is keyed to crystallization and his unhampered reign would result in cosmic in- eria, for he destroys action. He is symbolized as the reaping skeleton, for he governs the bones of man and the planets which are the bones of the Macrocosmic Man. He is the cold demon of ice that freezes the spirit in the blood and is given dominion over the tomb of unrealized hopes. He is the spirit that finally calls unto himself all things which have poured out through his mystic rings.

LUCIFER—MARS (*According to the Greeks, Venus*)

Lucifer, on the other hand, is the spirit of excess, the flaming son of rashness and the ruler of sense-gratifi- cation, over which he wields dominion with a sceptre of serpents. Those who fall victims to his power do deeds of violence, not because he wills it so, but be- cause they have this spirit of energy and pervert him themselves. Lucifer is the light-bringer; he is trans- muted by man into the fiery demon of war and hate. His power is used by man as the inspiration of lust and passion—while he would have it used only for the attainment of ideality. Uncurbed, those who fall un- der the sway of his influence, dash madly to their own destruction. He always is opposed to Satan, seeking to snatch the soul of man from the cold embrace of the Father. He is the heat that incubates the soul, but man uses him as a flame to burn up reason.

29. All the powers in Nature naturally serve good, but as they are the servants of those capable of wield- ing authority, man makes out of them barbarous spirits

who damn his own world. Between these two thieves of excess—Satan (utter coldness) and Lucifer (blazing heat)—hangs the spirit of man, crucified like the Christ of the sublime allegory, seared by the burning fire of one, chilled to freezing by the negation of the other. Here is the great truth. Suppose either of these forces which man has made into demons were to withdraw—what would happen to the Plan of Being?

30. If Satan were to go out of the scheme, man would be burned up by the fiery passions of Mars and the angels of Lucifer. Without the chill, caution, and curbing of Saturn, his soul would speedily be lost in utter debauchery and licentiousness. If on the other hand, Lucifer should withdraw, man would soon be a stone again, incapable of incentive, of motion or emotion, and chained, like the sufferers of Dante's Inferno, by the icy fingers of death.

31. Thus it is that the eternal battle of these great principles, like night and day, tempers the blasts and blends them to the good of man that he may ultimately reach the goal to which he aspires. Such is the mystery of night and day. If the sun were to shine all the while, man would be burned up with its rays and so vitalized that he would speedily turn into ether; while if night forever enshrouded him, he would gradually return to crystal.

32. Satan and Lucifer are not evil, but are two of the greatest powers in all creation. Without them the universe could not come into being—for Mars with the Lucifer angels is the dynamo of our solar system and without them the planets could not keep up their endless march. On the other hand, Satan builds the earth and worlds by his crystallization without which

we would have no solid substances to form bodies. It is not force or power, but the perversion of force which constitutes evil. The magician says: *"Demon est Deus inversus."* We may say: "The Demon is power perverted." Therefore man, the perverter of power, is the creator of demons, because he is the lowest creature capable of exercising authority from within his own being. The lower kingdoms are forced to react upon group impression and obey unquestioningly.

33. In *Paradise Lost* Milton tells how sin and death were launched into the world as the result of the disobedience of man. Satan, as prudence, negation, and crystallization, represents Death, who eternally inhibits his creation; while Lucifer as energy and action represents sin, the positive expression of misuse. They go about ministering to the needs of creation as constructive and helpful powers until the Black Magician, with the innate perversion of his own soul, bends them from their appointed way and launches them upon man as spirits of hell. The ancients called the forces of Nature the one-eyed gods because they were no respecters of persons, but fulfilled their appointed paths whether it be to kill or resurrect. The individualizing consciousness of the seven rings of sparks cast out from the universal Pralaya must become the one molder of these forces, and the Karmic responsibility for this molding and the expressions of these forces rest not upon the forces, but upon human and superhuman intelligences.

34. The Black Magician is one who learns to manipulate these forces for selfish and destructive purposes, his own aggrandizement or the fulfillment of desire, while the White Magician prays that he may learn to manipulate them as God would have them manipulated

—for the salvation of the divine creation. The powers are in the hands of those capable of invoking them, it makes no difference whether for good or ill. For this reason the schools of White Magic conceal these powers from man until through growth, purification, and unfoldment he gains the proper incentive for using them.

The Power of Black Magic.

35.   We must disabuse our minds of the idea that the Black Magician cannot injure us because we are in the right, or that he is weak because he is evil. This is a foolish concept taught to prevent man from strengthening himself and is propaganda of the Black Path itself.   It is just as foolish as to say that if a prize fighter were boxing a baby, the baby would win the fight because he has no ulterior motive, or because his soul is undefiled.   Thousands of people have not enough ambition to develop the necessary strength. In fact, they do not even know that their soul is worth saving.   They are living honestly, they are good Christian people, but so purely negative that they are positively advertising the fact that they are easy marks for anyone desiring to avail himself of the opportunity. They are not black themselves but they are the type that helps to make possible the perpetuation of Black Magic.

36.   That right will utimately triumph is undeniable and that the Black Magician will fall victim to his own excess is a literal truth, but many must bow their heads to the tyrant while he passes and only those who are strong are in safety.   Individuals who have mastered Nature's forces to such a degree that they can stop the heart-beat of a person on the other side of the

earth with a mental ray, or burn a two-inch hole through a foot and a half of ebony with astral fire, are dangerous wherever met, and the average so-called good person has absolutely no chance of withstanding the blows of Black Magic. Only fools underestimate this danger; wise men protect themselves against it, for an ounce of prevention is worth a pound of cure. The white ray places the shield of David between them and the dark forces and in this way they protect themselves.

37. We have reached a period in the history of the world when ignorance is criminal and deserves the heaviest penalty. Ignorance is not Black Magic but it is the greatest ally that the Black Magician has in the world today. People who do not know any better are constantly doing someone else's dirty work. That is the fruitage of their indolence. When we attempt to break Nature's laws, we tear down our bodies and render our consciousness negative, in this way opening those centers of our being through which we can be influenced and often obsessed by the black forces. This is almost as great a crime as perpetrating Black Magic yourself. People must realize that they cannot straddle the fence between right and wrong. They are either on one side or the other, and while doubt remains we can count them as being on the Black side, for doubt itself is an attribute of Saturn (Satan). Those who are not striving for the highest partake of the lowest.

38. Let us meet this problem fairly, neither with fear nor with too much confidence. In humility and contrition of spirit let us realize that the work being done in the world by the black forces all the time is very real. Recognizing this, let us band ourselves to-

gether and join in this righteous war, standing side by side with the Brothers of Light in the battle for human souls.

39. When light comes the shadow goes. Where the sword of enlightened spirit strikes, the hosts of darkness and negation are dissolved, but remove the light for only a second and they return as powerful as before. The powers of darkness work alike through the thoughtless and the silly, the arrogant and self-righteous and many of our most earnest truth-seekers are unconscious channels for the forces of evil, since in moments of weakness they allow the beast to attain mastery over them and through them to attack the world.

40. Learn to discriminate between light and darkness in the world you live in and watch your heart night and day that there may issue from it nothing that can be used as a weapon for the destruction of light. Do not worry over your past misdeeds—for worry itself breeds demons—but eliminate them from your aura, planting instead good seeds with constructive labors Feel your own personal responsibility in this problem, for the realization of responsibility is good for the soul. Demonstrate this acceptance of responsibility to the higher powers of Kosmos, for when your light shines out, the spirits of evil must slink into the corners and cover their faces with the shadow of their cloaks.

The Demoniacal Powers of the Ancients.

41. Let us now consider those strange creatures of other planes, some said to be souls lost from our own life waves, whom Black Magicians use in their conjura-

tions. Many of the transcendentalists of the past have forced these elementals and Nature spirits to serve them as in the days of the lost Atlantis. But the true Black Magician does not work through the ethers which are the home of the etheric elementals. He works through the entities who dwell in the astral light or the animal

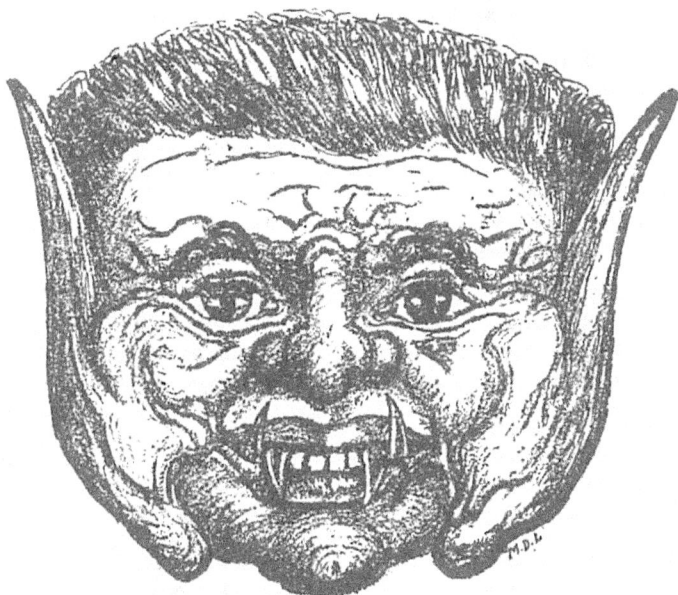

magnetism of the lower astral plane. The true Black Magician can become (and usually is) clairvoyant, but he can never go any higher than the astral world. To this plane he is tied by his passions, hates, incantations, and the animal nature which is the basis of Black Magic.

42. The ancients claimed that there was a hierarchy of demons for each of the sins of man and that in reality the demons were in most cases the incarnated

principles of these sins. By this it is understood that the animal excesses of man build on the lower planes of the astral world strange creatures, some resembling debased human beings, and others shaped like animals, lizards, snakes, and other reptiles. The power of the Black Magician lies in his ability to direct these soulless creatures, which, while not in reality individualized things, still have tremendous power over their own essences, both in the body of Nature and of individuals.

43. We seldom realize that our own passions and hates create these demoniacal beings in the superphysical world, but this is one of the secrets of Black Magic. Every evil or debased thought and emotion of man helps to build these tearing, rending creatures, the innate qualities of which become, in the hands of those who know, agencies for the destruction of the powers of light. It also seems part of the plan that those who chain these demons shall themselves fall victims to their own slaves, for one after another the Black Magicians are sucked into the maelstrom of the astral hell. The lower planes of the astral world are the three hells of religion and are the homes of these excess-created beings that battle and rend each other with never-ending fury.

44. The Black Magician, becoming a conscious channel for these forces, launches a stream of hell demons into the world. In so doing he sells his own soul (for these forces must pass through his own astral body) in exchange for the powers that these demons will give him over his fellow men. The powers of these elemental creatures are practically unlimited and there are many depraved souls who are glad to barter

A FIRE SALAMANDER

their immortal spirits for the power which these demons give them over the material world.

45. There are two kinds of Black Magicians: (1) those who use the demons of the astral plane for their villainy, which they invoke through necromancy and invocation; and (2) those who create their own demons and launch them against the world. The first group does the greatest harm to the world, but the second injure themselves more. The first group is composed mostly of conscious Black Magicians, while there are many in the second group who are totally ignorant of what they are doing. Some never learn their mistake until the demons they have created come back to the person who sent them forth.

46. The White Magician uses none of the powers of the animal world in his work, but rather seeks to transmute the poles of the beast within himself into higher and finer qualities. The White Magician labors entirely with the finer forces of the elemental planes. He is a builder—not a destroyer—and seeks to liberate rather than to dominate his fellow creatures. The White Magician has dedicated his soul to the immortal light, while the Black Magician has sold his for mortal glory. The *Grimores* of the Middle Ages are filled with chants and charms for the invoking of spirits. History is filled with stories of Black Magicians but the true student of occult science must have nothing to do with these things other than to protect himself against them.

Spiritual Research.

47. Do not experiment. In spiritual things experimentation is usually fatal, and unnumbered students have gone to untimely graves and lunatic asylums, or have become obsessed while they were trying some-

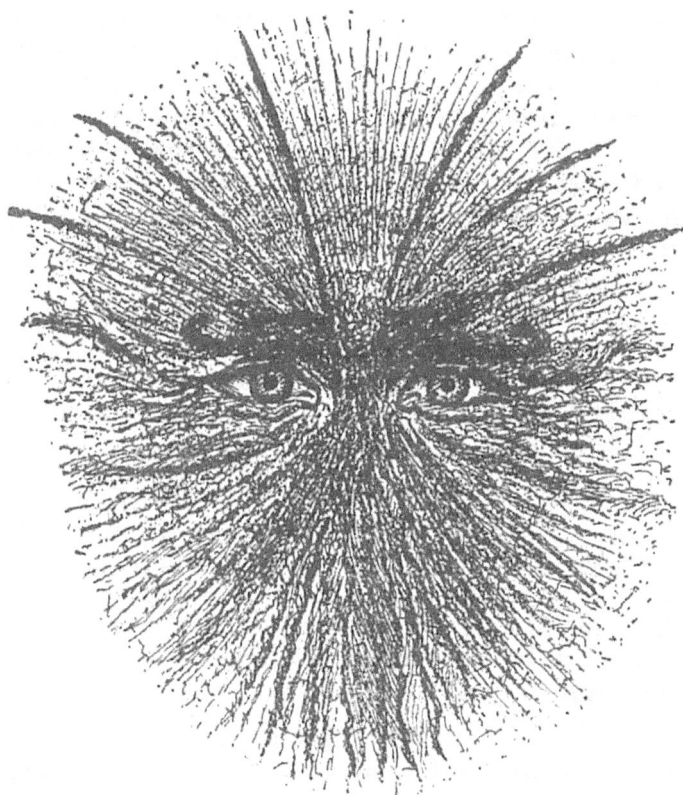

thing. Keep away from the phenomenalism; there is nothing in it for the true student. He is not seeking to gain salvation through his eyes but through his soul. Phenomenalism never appeals to the higher side of the nature but at most satisfies only inquisitiveness. As of old, so today, the cry is seldom "Save souls," but is usually "Show us miracles."

48. Have you ever felt that a person you have met is evil? Have you ever felt a strange repugnance for a certain person? These are the elementals and thought

forms which permeate the aura of the person in question. These elementals are drawn by the law of attraction. If you have similar qualities within your own soul, these creatures will leave others and flock to you to live like leeches off the best that is in you. Often when people leave a mediumistic seance, they carry away with them dozens of these demon forms that entered their organisms when they made their will power negative and thus opened the door. Others carry from the place many of these elementals who, unable to penetrate the aura of a positive person, still flutter around it awaiting the opportunity. The first time they lose their temper or do a destructive act, the door is opened and the elemental enters.

49. If any of these demoniacal creatures were to confront a person on the physical plane it would scare him to death, but because the unfortunate person does not see them he does not worry. It would be wise if people did consider them, however, as they will find out, if they do not fortify themselves by taking the White Path.

50. Man is a tiny germ floating on a sea of criss-crossing impulses and if he allows his own protecting aura to be broken down, these forces will rush in from every direction and so confuse and waterlog him that he will lose all chance for higher understanding. Idleness and negativity are cardinal sins and the Devil of all religions will find work for hands that are not laboring for the White Masters.

51. In this day and age the light must shine forth and the rulership of demons must be terminated. A large percentage of man's spiritual, intellectual, and physical affairs are today in the hands of elementals —brainless creatures—and their masters, the Black

30

Magicians, whose minds are dens of iniquity. Out of this world must come a few who with sincere hearts and souls undefiled will keep the light burning that the powers of darkness shall not triumph.

52. The false dominion of demons must fall, and with it the Goat of Mendes, the Prince Baphomet of the world. The false light and the false darkness must pass away that the light of truth and the true darkness may come into its own.

53. From the passions of man there pour into the world streams of living death. From the hearts and mouths of men sin and death are launched into being. These will go forth slaying and to be slain, bringing down upon civilization the curse of the gods. Black Magic will sink our continent as it has those that have gone before, for it launches upon us the furies of the elements and the holocausts of earth. Only one procedure can prevent this cataclysm. These demons must be starved, all passion must be transmuted into compassion, and the Black Magician must be brought into the light of truth that the law may be fulfilled.

Go Thou and Labor in the Vineyard.

In the Name of Jesus
Christ, Our Lord.

The End of the Second Instruction

31

DIAGRAM SHOWING HOW HEALTHY
VITAL BODY PROTECTS MAN FROM
BLACK MAGIC AND DISEASE.

PART THREE

The Mechanics of Magic

54. Man is composed of three principal parts: spirit, mind, and body. Body, in turn, is divided into vehicles and essences. The essences are divided into two distinct divisions: a distillation of body consciousness commonly called the soul, and the archetypes or molds. These molds are often referred to as patterns, trestleboards and architectural plans, after which the bodies are shaped and formed.

55. The vehicles or bodies of man are four in number, each having its respective mold into which it is cast while in a fluidic or mutable condition. These bodies are named the physical body, composed of solids, liquids, and gases; the vital body, composed of two atomic substances and two elemental essences; the astral or emotional body, composed of seven strata of volatile fire atoms called asteroids; and the mental body, composed of two major divisions designated as *rupa* and *arupa* by the Hindus, and more commonly known as the worlds of formed and unformed thought, or abstract and concrete mind. These four bodies constitute both the chain of vehicles which we know as the inferior nature of man, and the invisible causal bodies which act and react in or through physical substance. In India these bodies are called a string of beads through which the life thread or consciousness runs, connecting them all together. This thought is beautifully expressed by Krishna in the Bhagavad Gita.

56. From the Macrocosmic Man radiate the four areas of activity which result in the forming of the body chain.* From the mouth of the Adamic prototype was ejected Brahma, the mind-born, as a personification of the ancient element of air. Without the element of fire and light, its manifestion, air was colorless and was referred to by the ancients as the true blackness. This was called the Crown of Chaos by the great Robert Fludd. It is the true darkness which precedes light, and may be truly called the Womb of Cosmos. It should be remembered that this figure merely represents Brahma in the aspect of Shiva, or the creator of the form-world. He becomes the four-headed Cherubim described by Josephus, and also the Hindu Brahma in his four-headed aspect after his fifth head, *akasa*, had been destroyed by Shiva. In simpler words, the figure represents the lower planes of our planetary and solar systems—those rates of vibratory force which react tangibly or intangibly upon the substances cognized by intelligence, sense, or sensation.

57. We know that our scheme of worlds began as thought-forms, or, as science pleases to call them, dark nebulae. This darkness is the substance from which were differentiated the mind-bodies of the present human race. The word *substance* in this case refers to the intangible mass of mentoids which composed the mind-body of the archetypal Adam. At the present time the Lords of Mind, or the formless air *Devas*, function in bodies composed of this attenuated substance, which Herbert Spencer defines as the basis of thought power. It was from the darkness of this *primum hyle* that the visible universe was differentiated, when the

*See diagram on Page 7.

34

dark nebulae in the process of their strivings (to use the terminology of Jakob Boehme) were brought into visibility through the glowing light created by the friction of the dark atoms.

58. Thought awoke feeling, and the fire-worlds were born, and our system, celestial and terrestrial, existed as a flaming nebula. (The occult philosophers agree partly with the theory now known as the nebular hypothesis concerning the origin of solar system. They teach, however, that the planets are never actually thrown from the parent sun or nucleus, but really remain as individualizing centers within the auric body of the parent globe.) The fire-worlds, according to the Brahmins, were born from the arms and shoulders of the archetypal man, They were called the Red Sons, or the fire-born, and the twisting and seething of flame was considered symbolic of their strivings, They represent the astral or emotional body of man, for all of the fire in human nature is an expression of the eternal principle of fire in the cosmic man.

59. Feeling gave birth to impulse, vitality was established, and the brown man was born from the viscera of the divine prototype. He was the water-born. He was ordained to labor in the fields and stores, for he was the principle of strength and energy. Geologists know, and so do astronomers, that when the planets were in process of cooling, great clouds of mist surrounded the molten globe. This humid ether was regarded by the ancients as the veils of the World Virgin. Under its influences were individualized the moon-faced gods, or shades and shadows. It corresponds with the vital body of man. Finally the crystallization of humility resulted in the formation of the solid earth, referred to as the black man, often called in

35

India the *sudra*, or the creature born into slavery, doomed to live in chains until the night of the gods dissolved its shackles. This is the physical body of all things, which bears witness through its functions and powers to its quaternary constitution.

60. It is interesting to see how closely the mythology of the Brahmins coincides with the latest discoveries of science. In the ancient Buddhist hymns we find many references to the unfolding atoms. Thousands of years before the Christian era the Tibetans knew that an atom was a solar system, but because ideas were expressed symbolically, the Oriental minds have never received proper credit for their philosophical penetration.

61. As the universe began as a dark nebula of mind stuff, so man, the little universe built in the image of His Father and bearing witness to the functions of his creative pattern, also began his physical manifestation as a mineral thought-form. Later he appeared as a fiery plant, and gradually, after many ages of transition, this plant became a sacred animal composed of a body of humid ether. Later, like his celestial archetype, he incarnated into physical substance as a human creature.

62. As a thought-form, he had but one body; as an astral plant, he had two bodies, one composed of mind ether and the other of fire ether; as an etheric sacred animal, he added to these two a body of water ether; and as a human being, he adds a fourth composed of chemical dense physical ether.

63. Man remains in the physical world, according to the Ancient Wisdom, for approximately eight hundred earth lives, during which time he passes through an infinite diversity of human forms and environments,

and learns to master the various organic qualities from which dense physical vehicles are manufactured. His great work during that time is to master the element of earth, and gradually to incorporate into his water, fire, and air bodies the qualities and essences which he extracts from his experiences in substance.

64. Man still has the three higher bodies, which are invisible but nevertheless all-powerful. Without the vital body he would be a mineral, for the stones and metals have not individualized any of the vehicles above the physical dense structure. At the present time the fire, air, and water bodies of man are manifesting only through the physical (earthy) organism, where the air body gives the power of thought, the fire body the power of motion and emotion, and the water body the power of reproduction and growth. Therefore, while unseen, there are many manifestations and functions which bear witness to the power of man's invisible constitution.

65. Occultists call the dark air body the mental sheath, the flaming fire body the astral sheath, the humid water body the vital sheath, and the physical body the dense chemical sheath. These bodies, one within the other and interpenetrating each other, compose what the human mind recognizes as its vehicles of consciousness. Through the mental body, man secures that reflection and thought which make him greater than the animal; through the astral body he secures those qualities of motion and emotion—sense, color and feeling, and many other qualities—the expression of which makes the animal superior to the plant; through the etheric body he gains the power of reproducing his species and also the functions of assimilation and excretion, for in these things the plant

is greater than the mineral. Of course, the mineral, by its actual existence, proves its superiority over the myriads of swirling, gaseous, formless essences which have not yet even the power of appearing in the physical world.

66. Through the channels offered by this quaternary constitution the consciousness or ego (or spirit) views, cognizes, senses, and reflects upon its environments. The bodies may be called the hands and feet of spirit. They are tools by means of which the abstract workman produces a concrete result. The physical and etheric bodies may be called the feet, for they are the foundation and the base. The astral and mental bodies may be called the hands, for they are vehicles of attraction, repulsion, and ingenuity. The spirit, while superior to all of its bodies, is incapable of manifesting without its chain of vehicles. This divine spark must always be limited by the quality of its bodies. In all too many cases it is the servant of its own dependencies. Instead of ruling its world by apostolic succession, the spirit is generally bowed and broken by the endless demands of the lower nature. The appetites, desires, and selfish propensities cast the spirit into a dungeon, while a false and cruel monarch rules the empire in his stead.

67. Some of the ancient Greeks symbolized man and his body by the human hand. The four fingers represented the body with its four major divisions; while the thumb, which works with none of the fingers but is useful because it is against the fingers in all of its functions, is used to symbolize the consciousness. In Scripture it is stated that God has set Himself against His children. It is also interesting to note that man is the only creature that has a thumb work-

ing *against* the fingers. In even the highest simians the thumb works *with* the fingers, being in reality only an extra digit.

68. Some ancient students have even correlated the three phalanges of the thumb with the Trinity. The first (or distal) phalanx, including the nail, was held sacred to the Father, and its size and shape was used in determining will power; the second phalanx was considered when analyzing the mental and reflec-tive powers of the subject; while the third phalanx, which is usually large and forms part of the palm of the hand, when overdeveloped was considered a sym-bol of a strong animal or physical nature, being sacred to the Holy Ghost, or the East Indian Shiva.

69. These five parts—the consciousness and its four bodies—were symbolized by the five-pointed star, or pentagram. This was known to mediæval alchemy as the sign of the cloven hoof, and also as the star of Bethlehem. According to the Pythagorean system of geometry, the Masonic apron, with its four points or square and the descending point of its triangular flap, symbolized the same thing. The lower flap conceals the mystery of the murder of Hiram; the raising of the flap symbolizes his resurrection.

70. The average individual does not realize that life, consciousness, and intelligence are separate and apart from physical substance, merely functioning through chemical bodies during the temporary span which we call *life* in the chemical world. One of the great occult laws is that *to function in any sphere or plane of substance in Nature you must have a body sensitive to and capable of adjustment with that plane of substance.* The student must realize that each body is capable of domineering over the others, and also of

being dominated by superior or stronger forces. To abnormally develop any phase of the nature is to create a tyrant that, because of superior strength, will vampirize and tyrannize over all other parts of the nature.

71. It is the power given by wisdom and knowledge that makes the occultist superior to his fellow-man, his superiority being proportionate to his superior intelligence. In every walk of life the uninitiated will be comfronted with mysteries. To the average person the working of a gasoline engine is just as mysterious as calculus would be to a kindergarten child, but intimate relationship and study result in that familiarity which gives ease in handling and intelligence in directing. It has been well said that no man is a stranger to his own valet. The philosopher is a servant of God, and by perfect serving, soon becomes capable of thoroughly understanding the desires and dictates of his divine Master.

72. There is a real science even in pegging shoes. Only after years of apprenticeship can man hope to master any craft. In spite of the terrible caste system in India, it is interesting to note that an individual who excels even in the simplest thing is given recognition, and may mingle with those of superior caste. There are but few who excel in anything, while of mediocre people in all walks of life the number is legion. Have you ever watched an individual who is handling with impunity tremendous units of electrical energy? If so, you realize that knowledge is power. The electrician is safe, because he knows the laws governing the thing with which he is working; but, should the electrician become careless for a moment, or a person who knows nothing of electricity attempt to do the same thing, he courts instant destruction.

MAN AS THE SACRED FIVE-POINTED
STAR, WITH SPIRIT HOVERING
ABOVE.

73. The laws of Nature obey no man. They know neither virtue nor vice. Like the one-eyed Cyclopes of the Greeks, they are giants that fulfill their predestined work, unmoved by the right or wrong use of their forces. The wise man obeys the laws of the substances with which he works, and thereby causes these substances to work for him; but let him for one instant break the laws of the energies which he is controlling and they destroy him without compunction or discrimination.

74. An occultist is an expert in the science of life. As an operative magician, he is able to manipulate the forces of Nature to the gratification of whatever end he may desire—but woe to him if those ends are not in harmony with the natural plan! By means of his knowledge he may work miracles, like the magicians of India, but his feats are miraculous only to those who do not know as much as he does concerning the subtle forces of Nature.

75. The control which knowledge gives over ignorance on the spiritual planes of Nature is very much like the control that wealth gives over property in the physical world. Wealth may be a blessing or a curse; so may knowledge, which is mental wealth. The wise man will always be master of the fool, for he has a mentality which is capable of demanding respect, and the fool must bow down to that thing which he cannot comprehend. In every age a few have come into the realization of Nature's tremendous powers, and in one way or another, legitimate or otherwise, have become temporary wielders of the serpent scepter. As a man can steal money and remain wealthy until the law dispossesses him, so may a black magician steal a certain amount of divine power and manipulate it to

the gratification of his own ends until at last his misuse of power destroys him.

76. During the later Atlantean world, and again
in our own modern civilization, there have been and
are minds powerful but not virtuous. These two words
are not always synonymous. Some of these perverted
beings were actual demigods as glorious as Satan himself, but their misdeed and falsities sent them hurling
into oblivion like planets gone wrong. These demon
gods bred Black Magic (the perversion of power) in
the minds of men; and to this time it has remained
nurtured by man's besetting sin, selfishness.

77. Evil will never cease to exist until selfishness
and greed are overcome as factors in dictating the at-
titudes of men. It is the common thing for the concrete mind to sacrifice the eternal to the temporal.
Man, concentrating upon the limited area of the
known, loses sight of the effect of his actions upon the
limitless area of the unknown. Shortsightedness con-
sequently is the cause of endless misery. Moral shortsightedness results in vice, philosophical shortsightedness in materialism, religious shortsightedness in big-
otry, rational shortsightedness in fanaticism.

78. Wise is the man who serves the greatest end.
Whatever be the cost, the thing which men have called
harmony and which Nature knows as perfect adjustment, is worth all that must be paid for it. Adjustment is the establishment of harmonious relationships
between the universal planes of Nature and the centers
of body consciousness in man.

79. Selfishness promotes self-interest and self-gratification. Slowly the world about vanishes, the soul
lives more and more to the attainment of its own
desires, and before long the rule of Mammon is com-

43

plete in that life. This means that the best dies and only the shell of material personality remains. It means that the urge of aspiration is no longer felt and that the spirit, immortal and superior, lives as the drudge of appetites and the bondservant of an animal organism, doomed to martyrdom within the prison walls of perversion.

80. We live in an enlightened age in those things pertaining to the body but woefully ignorant concerning those things which are divine. Every day the spirit of commercialism is gorged with the life blood of millions. Every day the struggle of competition takes more of man's time and energy until the finer nature dies for want of consideration and virtue is deemed an impediment to the progress of the material Juggernaut. This turbidity of mental and moral outlook is the breeding place for the larvae of Black Magic, the curse of the human race.

81. Black Magic is a disease. It is a racial cancer. Its long tendrils are like those of an octopus. It infests church and state alike. It enters the hovel of the poor as false hope, leading him to crime and self-destruction. It enters the salons of the wealthy and as ambition turns the heart of man into a scheming organ for the accumulation of opulence. Black Magic is bred in selfishness, nursed by greed and tolerated only by hypocrisy, but nevertheless is a most common efflorescence of a commercial age.

82. Magic is not a mediæval superstition tutored by the spirit of ignorance: it is a very material fact. This so-called age of enlightenment is in reality only a transference of emphasis from one mental function to another; and while the spirit of arrogance and selfishness remains in the souls of men they will sell their

immortal spirits, as did Faust, for the gratification of self, or, more correctly, the not-self. Honesty is a jewel of priceless value, and the forces of evil have little power over a life lived true to principle. Man first by his covetousness must offer his soul for sale before the Devil is in position to buy it.

83. Nature is an endless area of criss-crossing energies. Those who have power can demand that these energies obey them, whether for good or ill, and senseless force must obey. But force also has its laws and penalties, and man must obey the laws of force or else suffer the consequences of his folly. The Black Magician in his selfish egotism thinks himself greater than God or law, and continually breaks the rules of force; but sooner or later, like Faust again, he is destroyed by his own servant. (We are told that Dr. Faustus actually lived in Germany in the early Middle Ages. He had a familiar spirit who served him. One day Dr. Faustus was found dead with a knife in his back, and the townfolk claimed that his elemental spirit had killed him.)

84. In our modern world, Black Magic finds a fertile breeding ground in man's desires. Age after age the wants of man destroy him. In ignorance he plays with fire, in thoughtlessness he ignores the immutable laws of Nature, and then wonders why the tempests break about his head, why lava and ash bury his cities, why wars lay waste his lands and mighty upheavals of the earth cause continents and nations to vanish in a single day. He neither obeys the laws of force nor recognizes that cause and effect rule all things; that day after day he reaps misery as the harvest of thoughtlessness.

85. The White Magician consecrates his life to

study, meditation, and service, that he may know the law and may direct force to its appointed ends. He molds himself into the Plan, becoming part of the divine rhythm by sacrificing himself and his wishes to the will of the Infinite, asking only to know wherein his duty lies and how he may be of the greatest service to the greatest number.

86. On the other hand, the Black Magician is firmly of the belief that he knows what he needs, when in reality he only knows what he wants. He seeks to mold the Plan into his own desires. He believes that the universe wants him to be greater than his fellow men, when the Cosmic. All does not know that he exists other than as a tiny atom passing with myriads of similar things to an appointed end.

87. Now let us see how the Magician, with his knowledge of the invisible side of Nature, is able to manipulate the unseen forces of Nature. First, the student must be impressed with the fact that the wise man is seeking to know what Nature desires him to do, while the foolish man knows already and tries to force Nature to act as the servant of his whims.

88. Nowhere is Black Magic more apparent than in the modern phases of religion. In both the new and old doctrines, instead of emphasizing the will of the Logos as the law of men, students have been taught to demand of the Infinite and that He will obey. No man may justifiably demand anything except the fruitage of his own labors. Today, however, millions are seeking by the route of psychology and metaphysics to reap where they have not sown, believing that the possession of a knowledge which makes them greater than their brethren entitles then to enslave the weaker and uninformed.

89. Let us now consider the four bodies of man as elements in Magic and differentiate clearly between the right and the wrong function of these bodies.

90. First, we will study the bodies as a group. We may say that they were created to be the helpmeet of their lord and master, spirit, for in truth they symbolize Eve taken from the side of Adam. The attributes of these bodies are legion, for each has a character of its own. We may say of the bodies of man, as of children: train them when they are young in the way that they should go, and when they are gray they will not depart therefrom. Our natures cannot be allowed to just grow, like Topsy, any more than children can be allowed to run around promiscuously and then be expected to amount to anything; our natures must be trained, and there must be a definite understanding who is master and who is servant.

91. A near-philosopher allows his mind to ramble, thus creating a host of abominable and absurd concoctions of witless thought. He involves himself and those about him in argument, dissension and never-ending streams of self-contradiction. He tries to solve the economic situation, creates new religions without learning the old, and buys his thoughts at pawnshops, his general purpose in life being to tear down something. He is like some of the writers of mediæval literature, who strove to give the impression that other authors were liars.

92. His mind, which should clarify the issues of life, does nothing but complicate them, and is used only as a means of finding gratification for the senses and thrills for the nervous system. His emotional organism is a mass of appetites and whims. He mistakes ambition for aspiration, cowardice for prudence, greed

for economy, and lust for love. So we may repeat, that through all this chain of bodies we see that the consciousness, instead of being clarified by its bodies, becomes more hopelessly involved by them every day. We may say, by way of definition, that White Magic is the service of the real. the consecration of life to the protection and unfolding of the real. It is the use of the forces of Nature for the good of all. Black Magic is the use of wisdom and its accompanying power to gratify sensation, ambition, desires, greed, and that medley of function which we call the personality. Its inevitable result is the destruction of the entire spiritual physical structure.

93. The White Magician seeks to gain control over himself. The Black Magician seeks to obtain control over others. Man has four centers of consciousness, four tangible assets, which he may consecrate to the attainment of reality: his mind, his heart, his vitality, and his physical body. A man may be forced to serve another, if that one can temporarily or permanently secure dominion over any of these four centers. To secure dominion over the physical body of another is to make that person a slave. To secure control over the vital body is to steal the vitality of another person, as in vampirization, where one person lives off the life essences of another. A common example of this can be seen when young people are brought up in the association of elderly people. The radiant energy of the child is sapped by the older person. As a result, such children are usually very nervous and seldom strong. Another example of the control of the vital system is to be found in mediumship, when decarnate spirits take ectoplasm from the spleen of a medium in order to materialize. This usually results in the nervous and physical exhaustion of the medium, for he has

given his own life as a vehicle to the outside intelligence.

94. The astral body is usually attacked through an excess of feeling, such as religious frenzy, grief, fear, or hate. When a person realizes that he can influence others while they are incapable of reasoning because of emotional excess, and awakens these emotional excesses for the purpose of influencing the weaker ones, as in the case of an evangelistic revival—such an instigating mind is a Black Magician. The sending of love, hate, or similar feelings to another, in the hope of awakening a similar condition in them for selfish or personal reasons, is also Black Magic.

95. Mental Black Magic is far more complicated, for it includes practically all prosperity metaphysics, autosuggestion, mental suggestion, occult treatments, demonstration over environment and conditions in people, hypnosis, mesmerism, personality culture, and other varieties too numerous to mention. In one way or another it includes practically all religious and economic graft, in fact every method in which the power of one person over another is used for the aggrandizement of the stronger. It covers every method of gaining superiority, except those based on an honest use of the merit system. Those who can do a certain thing better than others do not need Black Magic in order to excel at all. We find under perversions of this idea such business subjects as psychological salesmanship and the like. The systems advocated work admirably, but they bring endless sorrow to whoever attempts to use them.

96. People who use these false systems vindicate themselves for the most part on two unsound hypothesis: (1) that God has intended man to have whatever his puny intellect desires; (2) that man knows what he

needs. Both of these are false assumptions. Man was not intended by God to be rich, wise, beautiful, healthy, witty, of charming personality, or happily married. This does not mean that the Lord has any objection to his being any of these things or all of them. It merely means that if he desires these things he must go forth as Adam was directed to do, earning his bread by the sweat of his brow and not by the sweat of somebody else's.

97. The aura of man's consciousness is his dwelling place. It is his feudal castle. Though he be driven from his home, from his world, that is his sanctuary. None has a right for good or ill to enter that sanctuary, other than by the door, any more than one would have a right to enter another's house by the kitchen window. The door of sanctuary in this case is the physical world, because here all men have the privilege of knowing their opponent. Here all have an opportunity to struggle against the thing they do not desire. Here your brother has the privilege of rejecting your proposition, or of accepting it if such be his pleasure. He may let you into his house or keep you out, as he may see fit, for here at least there is one equality. Men may say "yes" or "no," according to their moral dictates, and may have the privilege of defending their integrity with their lives.

98. You may go up to your friend John and say, "I wish you would stop smoking; you ought not to do it." But you have no right, regardless of how virtuous or altruistic your desire may be, to sneak into the brain of John and implant there something which he cannot combat because he does not know that it exists. Any person who does such a thing assumes the responsibility for the life that he has lead out of its natural course.

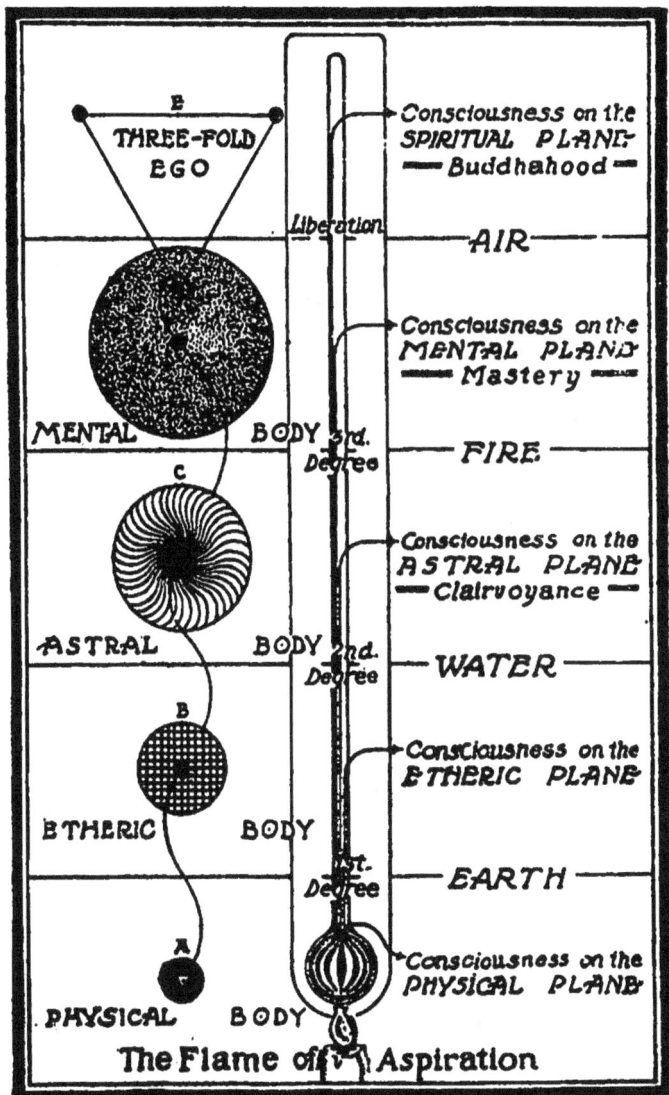

DIAGRAM SHOWING HOW CONSCIOUS-
NESS RISES THROUGHT THE FOUR
LOWER BODIES.

99. The Masters themselves, our Elder Brothers, will enter no man's house unless invited, for they accord all creatures the privilege of living their own lives. If an occultist were to break both legs and should ask in whatever way he knows that one of the great healers should mend his left leg, the healer would come, labor with that leg, and go away, even though he knew the right were broken also. He will not touch it, for he has been given permission to work upon only one.

100. Wisdom is given to no man until he asks for it, for in Nature every creature is accorded the privilege of unfolding its own destiny, guarded and protected legitimately by those intelligences placed there by Nature for that purpose. Those about us in the world who seek to assume the lives of others and set aside the low of individual completeness always injure and seldom do good.

101. An aged and wise Chinese once set out to visit a distant place. He sent a messenger ahead to tell the good folks of the house to prepare him no food save rice; but when he arrived, he found a many course dinner awaiting him, for the good family felt that they must so honor his presence. The philosopher reproved them, saying, "I asked for rice, you have given me fish; I asked for rice, you have given me corn; I asked for rice, you have given me meat; I asked for rice, and you have given me sweets; and among all these things you have given me no rice." Observing that the family was hurt by these words, the philosopher added: "I have lived these many years, and, after studying carefully this body which God has given me, I have found that it doth flourish nobly upon rice. It was with wisdom that I ordered rice; it was

with folly that you insulted me by offering other foods. You say that I am a great philosopher, that I am wiser than all other men; and yet you did not think me wise enough to order my own meal." In the same way when our brother asks for rice we have no right to give him meat because we think he ought to have it. It matters not whether the meat be physical or spiritual, whether the rice be literal or allegorical.

102. No man who is sick should be healed merely because he is ailing. He should learn the lesson that accompanies the disease that he has brought upon himself. To affirm health is foolishness; to find out the reason for the ailment, make right the wrong and become healthy again, is wise and proper. To be so moderate, so wise, so thoughtful as not to become sick, is still better philosophy. It is Black Magic of the worst kind to interfere in any way with the individuality and mental independence of any human being. If this individual becomes a menace to society, it may become necessary to incarcerate him for the good of the community, but this does not in any way interfere with the conscious functioning of his mind.

103. If the incident shows such a one the error of his ways, it is well; but whatever the result, he has been permitted to remain the maker of his own destiny and the captain of his own soul.He is at least living his own life and dying in the way that he chooses. He has been reasoned with and it has failed; he has scorned pleadings and prayers. All has been done that man can do. Let no one enter the sanctuary even of the criminal soul; for as his spirit is a part of God, endowed with the inalienable prerogative of choice, so the vengeance of God will descend upon him who seeks to steal in and cloud that brain or influence that divine spark

against its own will. Many an individual has played havoc with the laws of Nature by not allowing the individual to fulfill his own destiny.

104. We cannot always tell why souls come into the world rich or poor, some to grow strong and survive, others to become weak and succumb; but this we do know, that the law of Karma directs these things, placing each life where it will best learn the lesson needed for its growth. Some must learn in sickness and pain; others in laughter and joy. Some must learn to be exalted; others to humble themselves. But all are here to save their souls by the sweat of their brows; to knead the bread of their own existence, even though they must mix it with their own life blood.

105. What man of myopic vision dares to ordain health for the sick or illness for the strong? Who dares to say this poor man should be rich or this rich man should be poor? Does he know the reason for his coming? Does he know the virtues and vices which, lying hidden in the past, are the invisible causes of his present condition. Does he know the reason for the environment wherein he dwells, or the urges that have led him to his present state? If not, then he should be silent.

106. By this we do not mean that the world should be unsympathetic or unready to help. We do mean, however, that the help should be given and not forced upon the other. It means we should serve each other, help each other, and love each other; but we should never try to obtain the whiphand over another or over Nature.

107. What right has anyone to believe that man was born into the world to be happy? In the Arabian Nights it is written, "Happiness must be earned." We

are born with a divine birthright—a mind, a heart, two hands, and two feet. If any of these be missing at the time of our appearance, we have some other function proportionately developed to take its place. With these tools we may go forth and earn happiness, but we have no right to assume that someone is going to thrust it upon us. We have come here for experience, as a child who goes to school. We may be happy in our studies, or we may curse them all the days of our lives. The wise are happy in doing the thing that should be done. When we command the universe to make well the sick or to make the rich poor, we know not whereof we speak; for in our zeal and ignorance we may be doing an irreparable injury to the one we love, like a parent who cannot deny his children the sweetmeats that they want. In granting their desires, we endanger both their lives and their future efficiency.

108. Let us rather assist all to adjust themselves to things as they are, helping them to build a more noble destiny for themselves; not trying to give them something or force the unknown upon them, but rather assisting all to develop those faculties which will make them worthy to have the things which they desire and that great peace which all the world is seeking. When we ask the Infinite Father to give us those blessings which we lack, or to straighten the crooked paths wherein we walk, let us always add this stipulation to our endless string of desires: "Let these things be, if they are best for me; if not, Thy will, not mine, be done." Let us always qualify our will to achieve by such deference to the Divine will that alone does all things well. In this we make safe the course of our procedure. This humility will save us from the great Adversary who, under the guise of egotism, whispers

to us that we are greater than the Infinite. Time and time again, as Milton said, we are hurled flaming from the ethereal skies when we seek to be greater than that Power which is the Cause of all things.

109. We all want the good things of life, we all desire to be surrounded by friends; but we have no right to expect to attract any of these things except when our own lives have earned us the right to be honored, respected, and admired. The struggle of modern competitive ethics is very keen, but it offers to the winner a prize in keeping with the intensity of the strife. The environment of modern social conditions was created by human qualities and temperaments, and man has placed himself therein in order to learn how to adjust himself to its complications and uncertainties. The victory lies in the control he gains over himself, his viewpoint, his temperaments, and his idiosyncrasies.

110. Man has long considered happiness to lie in dominating others, or in keeping up with the standards of the Joneses. All through the ages he has striven either to imitate or control others, instead of acquiring self-control and unfolding the individuality which makes him different from all other things and gives him the power of excelling in something. When man exchanges his daily life of service for mental shortcuts, and excuses his vices instead of mastering them, he is falling under the influence of Black Magic, a subtle power which caters to the worst in him. People are eternally trying to *walk* out of difficulties, instead of trying to *work* out of them. The result is always fatal, for the problem evaded must be forever the problem unmastered.

111. In the frontispiece we see the auric bodies of man. In the center is the physical, the stone; above

and around this radiate the lines of force, which we call the finer bodies. These bodies are urges to mastery and also endless causes of slavery, depending upon whose shoulders the responsibility reste. Surrounding this black physical form is man's disease armor, called the vital aura, shown diagramatically in the drawing as a checkered area because of the interpenetrations and crisscrossings of the two higher ethers with the two lower. Under normal conditions this etheric body radiates through the pores of the skin in a form re- sembling fine fur extending several inches beyond the body. Occultism teaches that germs are more astral and metaphysical than substantial. As a result, while this vital aura radiates from the body, it protects man against evil forces and influences from both the physi- cal and etheric worlds. If he is run down, debilitated, or his vital forces depleted, this aura loses its power and allows a thousand external influences to tear down his strength and courage. It also permits disease elements to enter, and the result is often fatal.

112. Outside the aura is the egg-shaped astral body, with its center in the liver and its large end downward, surrounding the areas of the greatest sensation. It is ever changing in color, and through it pass endless shadow forms which express in panorama the emotions and feelings of man. It is glorious, radiant, opaline, never appearing twice the same. Outside this is the mental body, as it would appear in a highly developed adept, as an egg-shaped vehicle with its large end up- ward, bulging through the area of greatest intelligence. It is the midnight blue of the dark nebulae referred to on page 34. These bodies are visible clairvoyantly, (also physically with the aid of the Kilner screens) as interpenetrating globes of light, and constitute the

causal bodies lying behind the motion, emotion, and rationality expressed by the dense physical envelope. envelope.

113. At a point between the eyes in the forehead dwells the human consciousness, in the holy place of His tabernacle, enthroned among the globes which form His bodies. Man, by his actions, is gradually un' folding the possibilities lying latent in his physical body. By his conservation of energy he is gradually unfolding sequentially the centers of his vital consciousness. This end can be attained only through intelligent living, for the vitality is extracted from the atmosphere, from the sun's rays, from our food, and from other sources. Through gradual purification and regeneration of his emotions and feelings—control of his fire-mist body with its outbursts and excesses—man gradually raises the vibratory rates and unfolds the latent possibilities of the astral body, thus redeeming the animal soul. By his thoughts, ideals, and aspirations, aided by the twin faculties of logic and reason, man gradually gains control of that seething mental vortex which will later put him in harmony with the divine mind of the solar God.

114. The occultist is taught that the so-called worlds of Nature are the bodies of the Solar Man, and that each of these bodies corresponds with the lesser vehicles within man himself. Thus adjustment of his mental body to the mental plane of Nature makes him one with the mind of God, and all the other bodies follow in the same procedure.

115. Each thought, emotion, and action according' ly is important, bringing ever closer the day of individ' ual liberation. Any power or quality which paralyzes or even delays this process is detrimental to man, and

anyone who consciously seeks to improve himself to the detriment of his brother is unfit to live; yet such a system forms the keynote of modern ethics. If man would only learn to be honest, realizing that the universe is honest and that we are rewarded according to our motives as well as our works, we would rid the world of much that is undesirable.

116. Black Magic appeals to the mass mind. It appeals to the principles of our civilization. It offers something for nothing. As long as there is cupidity in the human heart, it will remain as a menace to the honesty and integrity of our race. If occult students will only remember that honesty is the deadly enemy of Black Magic and that it holds no terrors for the individual who is true to himself and true to the Golden Rule, he can protect his own soul and those he loves from its insidious and unnatural powers.

End of the Third Instruction.

www.ingramcontent.com/pod-product-compliance
Lightning Source LLC
Chambersburg PA
CBHW060638280326
41933CB00012B/2080